# Who Is Taylor Swift?

by Kirsten Anderson

illustrated by Gregory Copeland

Penguin Workshop

For Natalie and Nick—GC

PENGUIN WORKSHOP
An imprint of Penguin Random House LLC, New York

First published in the United States of America by Penguin Workshop,
an imprint of Penguin Random House LLC, New York, 2024

Visit us online at penguinrandomhouse.com.

Library of Congress Cataloging-in-Publication Data is available.

Printed in the United States of America

ISBN 9780593754221 (paperback)      10 9 8 7 6 5 4 3 2  WOR
ISBN 9780593754238 (library binding)   10 9 8 7 6 5 4 3 2  WOR

# Contents

# Who Is Taylor Swift?

It was the summer of 2006. A country music radio station in Nashville, Tennessee, was taking song requests from listeners.

The host answered a call live on the air. It sounded like a young girl.

"Hi, can you play that 'Tim McGraw' song you played earlier?" she asked.

Tim McGraw was one of country music's biggest stars, and he had a lot of hits, so the host asked the caller which Tim McGraw song she wanted to hear.

"The one by Taylor Swift."

Listening to the radio as she drove through Nashville, sixteen-year-old Taylor Swift screamed, "YES!" and nearly slid off the road. Someone had actually called a radio station to request her new song! Maybe her dream of becoming a country music star was coming true.

Even though Taylor was young, she had already experienced a lot of difficulties trying to break into the music industry. She'd been told that teens didn't listen to country music and adults wouldn't be interested in her songs. She'd walked away from a deal with a record company because she wasn't sure they would let her record her own music.

But Taylor felt that she had something to say. She knew there were plenty of girls who would be able to relate to her songs. They were trying to fit in at school and find friends, too. They were going through first loves and first breakups just like Taylor.

On that day, driving down a street in Nashville, she felt like she had taken a big step in her career. Then again, it was just one step. There was going to be a lot more work for Taylor and her team to do, but she was ready for it.

Taylor Swift planned to make music the focus of her life—and she would bring her fans along for the thrilling ride.

# CHAPTER 1
## Life on a Farm

Taylor Alison Swift was born on December 13, 1989, in West Reading, Pennsylvania. Her father, Scott, worked in banking. Her mother, Andrea,

had also worked in banking before becoming a stay-at-home mom. When Taylor was two years old, her brother, Austin, was born.

Taylor and her family lived on a Christmas tree farm that her father had bought from one of his clients. Every morning, Scott would get up early to do chores on the farm before heading into the office. The rest of the family pitched in to help with other tasks, especially during Christmas.

Taylor's job was picking the praying mantis eggs out of the trees so that they wouldn't hatch in people's homes! The excitement of Christmas on the farm gave Taylor a lifelong love for the holiday season.

The family kept horses on the farm, too, and Taylor began riding them at an early age. She competed in horseback riding tournaments, and her mother dreamed Taylor would become a champion rider when she got older. But Taylor was drawn to something else.

As soon as she could talk, Taylor began to sing. She plucked out tunes on toy pianos and learned all the songs from her favorite Disney movies. When she was six, her parents took her to see the young country star LeAnn Rimes in concert. Taylor was enchanted. She started listening to other popular country performers like Faith Hill, Shania Twain, and the Dixie Chicks (now known as the Chicks). Taylor was fascinated by the way country songs told stories. Sometimes when a song she liked ended, she would continue the story herself by singing verses that she made up.

Taylor performed in local children's theater productions. And when she was nine, she began taking singing and acting lessons in New York City. Her parents gave her a guitar, but it was too big for her, and she lost interest in it.

But Taylor still wanted to sing. She asked her parents to take her to restaurants that had karaoke contests, where people can sing along with the music track from popular songs. She found minor league sports events where she could sing the national anthem before a game.

That helped her get used to performing in front of big crowds. She even got to sing the national anthem in front of thousands of people at a Philadelphia 76ers basketball game! Taylor loved it when she sang and the audience applauded for her. She always wanted to please people.

By now, Taylor knew she wanted to become a country music singer. At age eleven, she begged her mom to take her to Nashville, the home of country music, so she could get a record deal. Taylor and her mom drove up and down the streets of Nashville's famous Music Row, where all the big record companies have their offices. At each building, Taylor dropped off a recording of

her karaoke performances. But none of the record companies were interested. Many producers and executives thought teenagers didn't listen to country music.

Taylor was disappointed, but she was not ready to give up. She now understood that getting a record deal wasn't easy. She needed to find a way to stand out.

During middle school, Taylor stood out in all the wrong ways. Her friends called her "annoying" and made fun of her for how much she followed the rules. Some days, no one at school would talk to her. When she sat down at a lunch table, girls would get up and walk away. Taylor often felt like the only friend she had was her mom.

But she knew she could always count on music to cheer her up. When Taylor was twelve, she started taking guitar lessons from a local musician named Ronnie Cremer. She fell in love with playing the guitar and practiced for hours a day. Then, Taylor began to compose her own songs.

She had always loved writing and poetry, so putting her words to music came easily to her. Taylor poured all the heartache and pain she felt from her struggles at school into her songs.

Taylor had been looking for a way to stand out from the other singers—especially those in Nashville. And now she had it. She wasn't just a singer. She was a songwriter.

# CHAPTER 2
## Taking a Risk

In 2003, Taylor signed with manager Dan Dymtrow, who had helped other musicians early in their careers. He got her some modeling jobs and helped her meet with important people at record companies.

Dan Dymtrow

When Taylor was thirteen, RCA Records signed her to a development deal. They would work with her for a year, and if they liked her progress, they might help her make an album. It wasn't a guarantee, but RCA was one of the biggest record companies in music. It meant that Taylor showed promise.

Taylor's parents realized that it was time to leave Pennsylvania. Her father transferred to his company's office in Nashville, and the family moved to a suburb outside the city called Hendersonville.

Taylor immediately felt happier attending Hendersonville High School. In Hendersonville, people didn't think there was anything odd about trying to become a country singer because many people there knew someone in the music business.

And on her first day of school, Taylor found
a best friend, Abigail Anderson. She often shared
her songs with Abigail before bringing them to
anyone else. It helped Taylor to be around people
who supported her dreams.

Abigail Anderson with Taylor

In 2004, Taylor made a big decision. Her deal with RCA was up for renewal. The company thought that she might not be ready to make an album until she was eighteen.

Taylor didn't want to wait four more years, so she decided not to renew her deal. This was a huge risk. Musicians all over Nashville would do anything for a deal with a big company like RCA. But Taylor just felt it wasn't right for her.

Instead, she went back to playing in talent showcases around Nashville. Taylor sent promotional packages with recordings of her music to record companies and music publishers. Although her deal with RCA hadn't worked out, it did help her meet people in the business and get a chance to perform for them.

One night in November 2004, Taylor's risk began to pay off. She got the chance to perform at the Bluebird Cafe, one of Nashville's most famous live music venues. Many popular country artists had gotten their start there.

Taylor performed three of her original songs that night.

In the audience was Scott Borchetta, an executive from Universal Music Group, another big recording company. Taylor had performed for him recently and mentioned her upcoming appearance at the Bluebird Cafe. After the show,

Scott Borchetta

he told Taylor that he wanted to offer her a record deal. However, he was planning to leave Universal Music Group to start his own record company and wouldn't be able to sign her until 2005. Taylor promised to think about his offer.

Meanwhile, Sony/ATV, a music publisher, had offered Taylor a contract as a songwriter.

Songwriters get paid every time their song is played or performed, even by other artists. Writing a hit song is one of the best ways to make money in the music industry. At Sony/ATV, Taylor would get to work with and learn from the company's many well-known songwriters. Taylor's new cowriters quickly discovered that she didn't need much help, though. One of her cowriters, Liz Rose, said she often just helped edit the songs Taylor had mostly written.

Liz Rose

Ten days after the show at the Bluebird Cafe, Taylor called Scott Borchetta and agreed to wait to sign with his new company, Big Machine Records. She thought that a small company would be able to pay more attention to her development as an artist.

Taylor used the time between making a verbal agreement with Scott Borchetta and signing her official recording contract to write more songs. One of these tunes came to her when she was sitting in math class. A boy she had been dating ended their relationship because he was going off to college. She wrote about the things that she hoped would remind him of her, including her favorite song by Tim McGraw. After school, she finished the song with Liz Rose.

After signing her contract in the fall of 2005, Taylor began recording her first album. On June 19, 2006, the record company released her song "Tim McGraw" as a single to radio stations. Borchetta knew it was a good song. He also knew the title would get people's attention.

One night Taylor heard it as part of a "song challenge" on a popular Nashville radio station. The station would play a new song, and then listeners could call in to say whether they liked it or not. Taylor sat nervously in her car with her friends, listening as callers voted. To her relief, people liked her song, and one listener even asked the radio host to play it again!

# CHAPTER 3
## The Best Day

Taylor receives CDs of her song "Tim McGraw"

Releasing a song was the easy part. Getting people to hear it took work. Taylor and her mom went on road trips where they visited as many country radio stations as possible. At each station, Taylor played her songs for the program directors.

Sometimes she brought homemade cookies to help win them over. Taylor even performed at small outdoor concerts where she had signs with her name on them.

Taylor also found a new way to reach more listeners. Myspace was an early social media platform that was popular with teens. Taylor used

it to post pictures, write about her life, and respond to questions. Before social media, it was very difficult for fans to connect directly with their favorite stars. By following Taylor's profile on Myspace, her fans could feel like they were her friends. Most record companies and older musicians didn't use social media at all. But it helped Taylor build a loyal fan base.

Taylor's self-titled first album was released on October 24, 2006. It sounded like traditional country music, with

guitars and banjos accompanying songs that Taylor sang with a country twang. But the songs were all about teen experiences, like having crushes and trying to fit in at school. By June 2007, the album had sold over a million copies.

In 2007, Taylor toured as the opening act for some of country music's biggest stars, including George Strait, Brad Paisley, and Keith Urban. Taylor even got to open for Tim McGraw and his wife Faith Hill!

Faith Hill and Tim McGraw with Taylor
at the Academy of Country Music Awards, 2007

After shows, she spent hours signing autographs for fans. Taylor's fans had developed a nickname: Swifties.

## Secret Messages

Taylor cares deeply about the words she writes, and she wanted to make sure that people would read them. From her first album to *1989*, she hid secret messages in the lyric booklets of her studio albums. Most of the lyrics in the booklets were written using lowercase letters, but some letters were capitalized. The capitalized letters spelled out names or phrases. Fans caught on, and it quickly became a game for them to decode the messages hidden in each song.  Taylor also puts clues and puzzles in her videos, social media posts, and even during her live performances. She said that she loves that her fans enjoy the guessing game. "Because as long as they like it, I'll keep doing it. It's fun. It feels mischievous and playful."

Taylor's busy schedule meant she had to be homeschooled. She did her schoolwork in airports or on tour buses. When she wasn't studying, she wrote and recorded new songs for her next album. There were thirteen songs on the album. Taylor liked to find symbols and connections in numbers, and her favorite number was thirteen.

*Fearless* was released on November 11, 2008.

Taylor explained that "fearless is getting back up and fighting for what you want over and over again . . . even though every time you've tried before, you've lost. It's fearless to have faith that someday things will change." *Fearless* was a huge hit, spending eleven weeks at number one on the *Billboard* 200 chart. Four of the songs from the original album reached the top ten on the singles charts.

Taylor began her first tour as the headlining performer in 2009, when she was nineteen years old. It was a big show, with dancers, sets, and costumes that matched the songs. But many of the most memorable moments were the simplest. During some songs, Taylor walked into the audience to greet fans. And throughout the show, her mom looked for the fans with the best signs, the most creative costumes, or just the most excitement. Those fans were brought backstage afterward for a "T-Party," where they had a chance to meet and take photos with Taylor.

T-Party with Taylor, 2009

In September 2009, Taylor went to the MTV Video Music Awards. Her hit song "You Belong with Me" was nominated for the Best Female Video award and she was scheduled to perform. Many of music's biggest stars would also be in the audience.

Taylor was shocked to hear her name announced as the winner of the Best Female Video award. She walked up to the stage and hugged the presenters before being handed her award. But just as she began her acceptance speech, rapper Kanye West jumped onstage.

He took the microphone out of Taylor's hand and announced that Beyoncé, another artist who was nominated for the award, had "one of the best videos of all time." He meant that Beyoncé should have won instead of Taylor.

The crowd booed Kanye loudly. But to Taylor, frozen onstage, it sounded like the entire audience was booing her. Maybe they agreed with Kanye. Maybe she didn't deserve to be there. Taylor was crushed. She slipped offstage quietly and cried with her mom. But she didn't have much time to recover because she had to go back out onstage to perform. Later, when Beyoncé won the award for Video of the Year, she invited Taylor onstage to finish giving her speech.

The event became huge news everywhere. Kanye apologized to Taylor through a public post on the internet, and the two spoke privately about the incident.

But the story wouldn't go away. Some people even argued that the embarrassing interruption had been good for Taylor's career. Before the show, she was mostly famous among country music fans and teen girls. Now, everyone was talking about Taylor and Kanye. Taylor was asked about it constantly, even when she said she didn't want to talk about it anymore.

The moment would haunt her for years.

# CHAPTER 4
## Jump Then Fall

Taylor's win and newfound popularity led to other opportunities. She wrote two songs for *Hannah Montana: The Movie* and got her very first professional acting role as a guest star in an episode of the popular television show *CSI: Crime Scene Investigation*. She played a rebellious teenager. This character had the complete opposite personality of Taylor, who was often cheerful.

Taylor acting in *CSI: Crime Scene Investigation*

And viewers were impressed by her acting skills. In the fall of 2009, she filmed a role in the movie *Valentine's Day*, and wrote a song for the soundtrack as well.

*Fearless* won Album of the Year at both the Academy of Country Music and Country Music Association awards in 2009. Then it won four Grammy Awards in 2010, including the night's biggest honor, Album of the Year.

Taylor holding her Grammy Awards, 2010

For Taylor, that was a dream come true. But it wasn't all perfect. During a duet with rock legend Stevie Nicks at the Grammys, Taylor sang off-key. Afterward, people talked about how bad she sounded. One music critic who had never liked

Taylor's voice said it proved his point that she couldn't sing.

It wasn't the first time people had noted that Taylor didn't have a strong singing voice. She knew that she didn't have the range or power of other singers, so she had always defended herself by saying she was a songwriter first. Her voice was just a way to tell her stories. But instead of feeling sorry for herself, Taylor used the harsh words as motivation and got more vocal training to help build strength and learn how to use her voice better.

Taylor also knew that many people in the music business didn't believe that she really wrote her songs. They thought her cowriters did most of the work. So for her next album, Taylor decided to write all the songs herself. The song "Mean" was a response to the critic who complained about her voice. In "Back to December," she wrote about mistakes she had made in a relationship.

Taylor named the album *Speak Now*. In the liner notes for the album, Taylor explained how she regretted not speaking out about her feelings at different times in her life. She encouraged her listeners to not make that same mistake.

*Speak Now* was released on October 25, 2010. It spent a total of six weeks at number one on the US *Billboard* 200 chart.

People praised the songs on *Speak Now*. But the lyrics in many of the songs also set off a guessing game among listeners.

On her first albums, the boyfriends and crushes Taylor wrote about were mostly people that she knew from high school. But now Taylor was spending time around famous people in Hollywood. She became friends with popular actors like Selena Gomez and Emma Stone. In 2008, she dated Joe Jonas, a member of the Jonas Brothers band and a Disney musical star. She had included a song on *Fearless* about how he had broken up with her in a brief phone call. *Speak Now* had more songs about Joe, as well as Taylor Lautner, a young movie star she'd dated while filming *Valentine's Day*. "Dear John" was a bitter song that was widely believed to be about Taylor's brief relationship with John Mayer, a much older singer-songwriter.

Taylor and Selena Gomez

Taylor didn't think this was a big deal. She even joked about it during the *Fearless* tour and while hosting an episode of the comedy sketch show *Saturday Night Live*. Male songwriters had always written about their romances. Taylor felt she was just writing honestly about her life.

Taylor hosts *Saturday Night Live*, 2009

Many parents saw Taylor as a role model. She was polite and didn't struggle with addiction or difficult behavior like some other teen celebrities. Parents felt it was okay for their kids to listen to her music and go to her concerts because she was seen as a nice girl.

She tried to be perfect. But it wasn't easy. Taylor worried about how her actions affected her young fans. She felt responsible for them and feared making mistakes. It was a lot of pressure for one person to handle.

# CHAPTER 5
## Love Stories

The *Speak Now* world tour launched in February 2011 and ran through March 2012. Different musical guests often appeared at the shows to sing with Taylor, including Selena Gomez, Hayley Williams, Justin Bieber, Nicki Minaj, and Usher. Before every show, Taylor wrote lyrics from a song on her arm.

Some were just lines she liked from her favorite songs. Others were chosen to fit her mood that night. Fans had fun trying to guess the meaning. She also continued the "T-Party" meetings after each show.

For her next album, Taylor wanted to try a new sound. While she recorded some country-style songs, she also decided to work with record producers who had helped create pop hits. Record producers supervise the recording of a song. They help musicians choose the beats, instruments that will be played, and effects that can be added to a recording. A record producer can change the way a song sounds.

Taylor called the album *Red*, because she said it was about strong or "red" emotions. Many of the songs dealt with a difficult romance that ended badly. Fans guessed that it was mostly about Taylor's short relationship with actor Jake Gyllenhaal.  Taylor called it her "only true breakup album."

*Red*, released on October 22, 2012, became

Taylor's third straight number one album. The song "We Are Never Ever Getting Back Together" was Taylor's first number one song on *Billboard*'s Hot 100 chart. The *Red* tour ran from March 2013 through June 2014.

Although *Red*'s most successful songs were pop hits, Taylor was still considered a major country star. At the Country Music Association Awards in the fall of 2013, she was given the Pinnacle

Award, country music's highest honor. The award had only been given out once before, to singer Garth Brooks.

In October 2013, Taylor attended the opening of the Taylor Swift Education Center at the Country Music Hall of Fame and Museum in Nashville. Taylor had donated $4 million to help create a learning center within the museum.

The center includes exhibits about music and classes for students to learn about songwriting and playing musical instruments.

Taylor was one of the most famous singers in the world, but she tried to have a normal life. She still made time for her friends, including her high school best friend, Abigail. A well-known lover of cats, Taylor shared pictures and videos of her cats on social media. One was named Meredith Grey, after a character in one of her favorite shows, *Grey's Anatomy*. The other, Olivia Benson, got her name from a character on another television favorite, *Law & Order: SVU*.

Taylor also enjoyed meeting and dating new people. She briefly dated Conor Kennedy, a member of the famous Kennedy family, and One Direction singer Harry Styles. She thought that it was normal for a young woman in her early twenties to date different people.

Taylor and Harry Styles

But for many, Taylor's dating had now become a source of entertainment. Talk-show hosts made rude comments about how many men Taylor had dated. Comedians and award-show hosts warned men to stay away from her because she might write a mean song about them!

Taylor was deeply hurt by this. She wanted to be known for her songwriting, not for who she'd dated. This was the first time she had been attacked for her personal life. But it wouldn't be the last.

# CHAPTER 6
## Welcome to New York

Taylor had lived in Nashville since she was fourteen. In early 2014, she decided she needed a change, so twenty-four-year-old Taylor moved to New York City.

Because photographers followed Taylor everywhere, she hired full-time bodyguards to protect her. But she still tried to enjoy city life as often as possible. Taylor was frequently seen in restaurants, out shopping, or going to the gym. She cut her long, wavy hair to shoulder length. She hung out with models like Karlie Kloss, Gigi Hadid, and Martha Hunt, and young Hollywood stars like Selena Gomez and Hailee Steinfeld.

They were photographed together constantly. People called them Taylor's "squad." Taylor had never forgotten how she felt in middle school when people bullied her or didn't include her. She was excited to have so many friends.

Taylor wanted to experience all the wonderful things the big city had to offer, but she knew eyes were always on her. Sometimes websites would post pictures where Taylor thought she looked overweight. She began to skip meals or work out for longer stretches of time if she felt she had eaten too much. Often during shows she found herself running out of energy because she hadn't eaten enough. She told herself that she was okay. But she wasn't. Taylor was struggling with an eating disorder. Like many people with eating disorders, she didn't recognize that she had a problem and was living an unhealthy lifestyle.

As always, though, Taylor found peace in her

music. In addition to moving to a new city, she decided it was time to fully move away from country music. Taylor's new songs were filled with electronic sounds that were popular in the 1980s music she loved. Instead of fiddles and banjos, Taylor's songs featured synthesizers and drum machines. She called the album *1989*, after the year of her birth. She said it was a rebirth of herself as an artist.

From September through October 2014, Taylor held a series of "secret sessions" for *1989*. In Nashville, Los Angeles, New York, Rhode Island, and London, superfans were invited to a location where they got to meet Taylor and listen to *1989* for the first time. At each session, Taylor served pizza and homemade cookies. She talked to each person and took photos with them.

It gave Taylor a chance to show her gratitude and help build excitement for the album.

On October 27, 2014, *1989* was released.

It quickly shot to the number one spot on the *Billboard* charts, selling millions of copies. The success of *1989* came during a difficult time for the music industry. Instead of buying physical albums, listeners were using music streaming services that allowed them to listen to any songs by any artists. Although these streaming services offered special listening options that required users to pay a fee, most of the services had a basic listening option that was free. When musicians were paid for digital streams of a song rather than the sale of a physical album or single, they earned less money.

Taylor challenged this system. In early November, she removed all her music from Spotify, one of the biggest streaming services. She argued that the company had a system that paid artists less for their music. In June 2015, Taylor announced that she would keep *1989* off another streaming service, Apple Music, because they weren't paying artists fairly. Apple quickly changed its payment method, and Taylor agreed to keep her music on it.

Taylor faced a more personal challenge in 2015. In April, her mother was diagnosed with cancer. Andrea successfully completed treatment for her cancer, but it was a big scare for Taylor. She considered her mother her best friend and wanted her around for as long as possible.

In May, Taylor released a video for her song "Bad Blood." In the video, the twenty-five-year-old star and her squad of famous friends acted out a story about a friend who betrayed Taylor. It was filmed like an action movie, and it won the Grammy for Best Music Video.

Scene from "Bad Blood" music video

When asked by reporters, Taylor hinted that the song was about a real friend's betrayal. Fans used clues to guess that Taylor was talking about singer Katy Perry. Later, Katy explained that some dancers who she usually worked with had gone on one of Taylor's tours. But when Katy began preparing her own tour, the dancers told Taylor they were going to leave her tour to practice with Katy. Katy thought it was okay that they came back to her. But Taylor seemed to think Katy was trying to ruin her *1989* tour.

Katy Perry

Some people questioned Taylor's actions. Taylor had said that she believed in supporting other women. Yet she had written a song and made a video about getting revenge on an ex-friend over a simple misunderstanding. That wasn't support. That was hurtful. For some people, Taylor and her squad just looked like a group of mean girls.

Still, most things were going well for Taylor. Her decision to leave country music and focus on a pop sound had worked well for her. She was one of the most popular entertainers in the world. In an October 2015 interview she said, "There's nothing I would change about my life."

# CHAPTER 7
## Antihero

Taylor's 2016 started out well. She won several Grammy Awards in February, including Album of the Year for *1989*, making her the first woman to win that award twice as a solo artist. But a few days before the award ceremony, Kanye West had performed his new song "Famous" at a fashion show. In the song, he took credit for making Taylor famous and used words to describe Taylor that upset her. After she complained about his lyrics, Kanye told the media that Taylor had a conversation with him before the song was released where she approved the words. Taylor's managers said Kanye had only asked Taylor if she could release the song on her Twitter account. Taylor had said no.

When Taylor accepted her Grammy Award for Album of the Year, she used her speech to tell women that they should not let men take credit for their work. She was clearly speaking about Kanye's claim that he had made her famous.

By early June, Taylor had broken up with Scottish DJ Calvin Harris and had begun dating British actor Tom Hiddleston. Photos of the new couple quickly appeared everywhere, leading suspicious people to claim the relationship was fake. They said Taylor was just trying to distract people from the Kanye West story.

Then things got even worse. In April, Calvin and popular singer Rihanna had released a song called "This Is What You Came For." The songwriters were listed as Calvin Harris and Nils Sjöberg. But on July 13, a news report came out revealing that Nils Sjöberg was really Taylor. She had written the song under that name because she wanted people to talk about the song, not her relationship with Calvin. But Calvin thought Taylor had leaked the information on purpose. He complained on social media that Taylor was trying to take credit away from him.

July 16 is World Snake Day. In July 2016,
Kim Kardashian, Kanye West's wife at the time,
called Taylor a snake on social media. Then she
released a three-minute clip from the call Kanye
had made to Taylor about his song "Famous." In
the clip, Taylor seemed to be okay with the words
Kanye wanted. She even thanked him for asking
her first.

Taylor responded that the clip only showed
a small part of the phone call. She said that the
words he used in the song were different than
what she had agreed to.

But some people did not want to listen to her. They began to call her a snake. They said she was cold-blooded. She planned everything to make herself look good and others look bad. They claimed she was always trying to get attention. Commenters posted snake emojis all over Taylor's social media pages. The hashtag #TaylorSwiftIsOverParty was trending on Twitter. Articles with titles like "When Did You First Realize Taylor Swift Was Lying to You?" began to appear all over the internet.

Taylor was crushed. She had always tried to make people like her. Now the whole world seemed to dislike her. In August, she wrote in her journal, "This summer is the apocalypse." It felt like the end of her world.

In the fall of that year, Taylor began to date British actor Joe Alwyn, and they agreed that it would be better for their relationship to keep it private. Their relationship lasted six years.

Taylor with Joe Alwyn, 2020

Taylor performed at events in October and in February. But after that, she seemed to disappear. She was rarely seen in public. She didn't post on social media or do interviews.

In August 2017, Taylor finally reappeared, but it wasn't for a performance or an album announcement. She had to go to court.

During an event with a radio station in 2013, a DJ named Dave Mueller had touched Taylor in a way that made her feel uncomfortable. She reported him to his bosses, and he was fired. In 2015, he filed a multimillion-dollar lawsuit against Taylor, claiming she had ruined his career. Taylor sued him back—for one dollar. She testified in court about what had happened and won the case. Taylor said she hoped it would encourage other women to take action when someone hurt them.

Later in 2017, the "Silence Breakers" who had spoken out about being assaulted were named *TIME* magazine's Person of the Year. Taylor was one of the women who represented the silence breakers on the magazine's cover.

On August 18, Taylor deleted all her old social media posts. Her website became a black screen. Next, she posted a video of a snake on Twitter.

A few days later, Taylor announced her new album. It was going to be called *reputation*.

# CHAPTER 8
## Look What You Made Me Do

Taylor didn't do any interviews to promote her new project. Instead, she just held secret listening sessions for fans similar to what she had done for her *1989* album. She also quietly returned all her music to Spotify.

Taylor released *reputation* on November 10,

2017. It was very different from her other work. It had some of the elements of electronic dance music that Taylor used in her previous album, but this collection used more hip-hop beats. In some songs, Taylor played the part of the cold-blooded "snake" that she had been called in 2016. The lyrics told stories about being bad and causing trouble. But other songs on the album were more hopeful. They focused on finding love and peace.

Taylor's album *reputation* debuted at number one on the US *Billboard* charts. It became the best-selling album in the United States in 2017.

Taylor began the *reputation* stadium tour in Arizona on May 8, 2018. The show had dramatic lighting and big dance numbers. A giant, inflated snake filled the stage for part of the show. But there were quieter moments, too, where Taylor just played the guitar or piano as she sang. She spoke honestly to the audience about her feelings and told them how grateful she was for their support. And after each show, Taylor still met privately with a group of fans.

The tour ended in Tokyo in November 2018, with the shows having been seen by more than 2.5 million people. Anyone who had thought Taylor's career was over in 2016 had clearly been proven wrong.

After the tour, Taylor felt better than she had in years. She had stopped worrying about her weight and was healthier. She had learned that she couldn't please everyone. The only people who mattered were the ones who truly cared about her. And Taylor now knew that if something bad happened to her, she could come back from it.

Taylor also finally felt strong enough to speak out about important issues. During the difficult 2016 presidential election, many celebrities had publicly supported one of the two main candidates. Taylor had not, and people criticized her for staying silent. They argued that if Taylor had supported a candidate, many of her voting-age fans would have registered to vote. Some people even said maybe Taylor could have changed the results of the election.

Taylor had grown up in the country music world, where musicians were told to stay away from politics. Country stars were warned that they risked angering half their audience if they chose a candidate. The Chicks had lost many of their fans after they criticized President George W. Bush.

But Taylor felt she had to say something and speak now. An important senate race was taking place in Tennessee in 2018. Taylor saw that the Republican candidate, Marsha Blackburn, had voted for laws that hurt the queer community and voted against laws that protected women from violence. (*Queer* is a term that can be used to describe anyone who isn't cisgender and/or is not solely attracted to people of the opposite sex.) Taylor decided to make a statement against Blackburn. She wanted to announce that she was supporting Blackburn's opponent, Democrat candidate Phil Bredesen.

Taylor's management team was against her plan. They worried that she could lose fans. Her father feared that it might put Taylor in danger. But she felt like she needed to do something.

In October 2018, Taylor put out an Instagram post explaining her decision. She also encouraged people to register to vote. In the twenty-four hours after her post appeared online, sixty-five thousand people registered to vote.

Taylor was disappointed when Blackburn won the race. But she felt freer now and was glad she had stood up for what she believed.

Taylor decided to leave Big Machine Records when her contract ended in 2018. Before leaving, she tried to buy her master recordings from the company. Masters are the original recordings that all future album copies are made from. The owner of the masters holds the copyright to that recording. Performers, songwriters, and song owners earn money each time a song or album is played on the radio or a streaming service. But the owner of the master gets the largest amount of money. The master's owner also gets paid if the recording is used in movies, TV shows, or video games.

Taylor owned songwriting credits on her music. But she wanted the masters, too. She felt like those recordings told her life story. They were personal. In the end, she couldn't make a deal with Big Machine, and they held on to her masters. In November 2018, Taylor signed a record contract with Universal Music Group. This contract allowed her to own the master recordings for her new albums. Taylor was taking control of her future.

# CHAPTER 9
## Miss Americana

In early 2019, Taylor had a chance to film a role in the movie version of the classic musical *Cats*. It was a perfect fit for this cat lover!

Cast members attended "cat school" before filming. They spent hours practicing how to move like a cat and learning how cats think. Taylor also got the opportunity to cowrite a new song for the movie called "Beautiful Ghosts" with the musical's composer, Andrew Lloyd Webber.

In April 2019, Taylor released a video for her new song "ME!" In one part of the video, Taylor holds a kitten. While filming, she fell in love with the kitten and adopted him, naming him Benjamin Button.

In June 2019, Big Machine announced that the entire record label and all of Taylor's masters had been sold to a company owned by Scooter Braun. Scooter managed several successful musicians. Taylor was horrified. She felt that

Scooter Braun

Scooter had been one of her worst bullies in 2016 because he had publicly taken Kanye's side that year. Knowing that Scooter would now earn money from her past work hurt Taylor badly.

On August 22, 2019, she struck back. She announced plans to re-record all the albums she had made for Big Machine. Taylor hoped that people would listen to her new versions more than the old ones.

The next day, Taylor released *Lover*. She called it "a love letter to love itself." With this album, she returned to creating

lighter-sounding pop music after *reputation*'s darkness and heavy dance beats. *Lover* became the best-selling album of 2019.

In January 2020, *Miss Americana*, a documentary about the past few years of Taylor's life, premiered at the Sundance Film Festival in Utah. The film gave a glimpse into Taylor's feelings and songwriting skills. It also showed Taylor speaking for the first time about her former problems with body image and the unhealthy relationship she had developed with food. Experts on eating disorders praised Taylor's honesty and hoped it would encourage others experiencing similar problems to seek help.

Taylor planned to go on tour in 2020, but she chose to make the tour much shorter than usual because her mother's cancer had returned. Taylor wanted to be near her as often as possible.

# Re-Recording

Taylor Swift isn't the first musician to re-record her music in order to own the masters. In 1960, famous singer Frank Sinatra started his own record company. He decided to re-record his songs for his new label so he would earn money from them. Country star Reba McEntire and rock band Def Leppard have also re-recorded their music as a way

to own the masters. Many artists have re-recorded their songs when a movie or TV show asks to use it.

Reba McEntire

But Taylor's plans changed drastically. In March 2020, a deadly new virus caused the COVID-19 pandemic, which shut down most forms of travel. Government officials required people to stay indoors to prevent the further spread of the disease. Like everyone else, Taylor followed the rules and stayed at home. She watched old movies and read classic novels. When she saw some of her fans post about their financial struggles on social media, she sent money. She also donated to food banks that were helping Americans who'd lost their jobs due to the pandemic.

During the early days of the pandemic, the complete recording of Taylor's 2016 phone call with Kanye West was released. It showed that Kanye had lied about Taylor giving him permission to call her harmful words. But Taylor had long since moved on from it.

On July 23, 2020, Taylor surprised the world

by announcing that she planned to release her eighth album that night at midnight. She said it would be called *folklore*.

It was unlike any of Taylor's other albums. Usually, she wrote songs about her own feelings and experiences. This time, many of the songs were stories about characters she'd invented. The background instruments used on the songs were mostly guitars and keyboards. It sounded more like quiet folk songs than pop or dance music. Taylor had recorded it remotely, working with other producers and composers through virtual video calls and recording sessions. Then, on December 11, just two days before her thirty-first birthday, Taylor released another album. Like *folklore, evermore* told stories about different fictional characters. Taylor said that after finishing *folklore*, "We just couldn't stop writing songs. . . . So I just kept writing them." In March 2021, *folklore* won Album of the Year at the Grammy Awards. Taylor became the first woman to win the award three times, breaking her own record.

Soon after, in April 2021, Taylor released the first of her re-recorded albums. *Fearless (Taylor's Version)* showed her approach to the project. She tried to record the songs the same way she'd recorded the originals. She only made changes when necessary. And she included six new songs. These were songs that she had written while originally recording *Fearless* but hadn't been able to fit on the album.

Taylor followed that up in November with the release of *Red (Taylor's Version)*. The biggest change was in the song "All Too Well." The original had been less than six minutes long.

The new recording was ten minutes, and Taylor directed the music video for it.

It seemed like Taylor's music was everywhere in 2022. But Taylor herself made very few appearances. She showed up at the MTV Music Awards in August. As she accepted the Video of the Year award for "All Too Well," she made a surprise announcement. Her next album would be released in October.

# Giving Back

Taylor has earned a lot of money in her career, but she also gives back to those in need. She helped buy a house for a fan who was homeless and pregnant. She sent money to one fan to help pay for college tuition and gave another fan $1,989 toward her student loan debt. She donated $15,500 to help the family of a fan whose mother was in a coma. She paid for a service dog for a fan with autism and gave $10,000 toward another fan's cancer treatment. She has given hundreds of thousands of dollars to cancer research.

Taylor has also donated to groups that help people who are affected by sexual assault and domestic violence. She has given money to the fight for queer rights.

And, of course, Taylor has given money to cat rescue groups and animal shelters.

Taylor Swift
6/11/1
St. Jude
$ 25,000
Twenty-five thousand
A M Entertainer of the Year

# CHAPTER 10
## Taylor's Version

Taylor said the songs on her new album, *Midnights*, came from the question "What keeps you up at night?" The resulting album showed that even successful people can struggle with self-doubt.

On November 1, 2022, Taylor announced her first tour since 2018. It was called the Eras Tour, and each of her albums represented a different era, or period, in her career. Tickets for the Eras Tour were set to go on sale on November 18. But fans who signed up for a special code could buy tickets on November 15. That day, millions of users tried to get tickets through Ticketmaster, an online ticketing website, but the site crashed due to all the traffic. Many of the tickets went to professional resellers, who sold them back to fans for extremely high prices.

The ticketing disaster caused some fans to sue Ticketmaster, and the US government began an investigation into Ticketmaster's control of the ticket sales industry.

The tour officially began in March of 2023, with Taylor playing several songs from each era of her long career. She played songs like "Tim McGraw" and "You Belong With Me" from her country-music era, "Shake It Off" and "We Are Never Ever Getting Back Together" from her pop-star era, and ". . . Ready for It?" from her edgy, dark era. The show became one of the biggest events of 2023. For many young fans, it was their first chance to see Taylor live. Fans who had grown up with Taylor now brought their kids.

People lined up outside the stadiums for days just to get a chance to buy the tour's official merchandise. Those who couldn't get tickets gathered outside the stadiums to listen and sing along with their favorite musician. It was a chance for longtime fans to meet up again, and for new fans to make friends. The show seemed to bring everyone together.

On July 7, 2023, Taylor released *Speak Now (Taylor's Version)*. The album went to number one on the *Billboard* charts, joining *Midnights*, *folklore*, and *Lover*. Taylor became the first woman to have four albums in *Billboard*'s top ten at one time.

Taylor has had a huge impact on the music industry. She used her songs, tours, and social media posts to develop a personal connection with fans. In response, her fans have shown incredible loyalty to her. Taylor's battle with Apple Music changed the way the streaming service pays musicians. The success of the *Taylor's Version* albums has shown other artists the importance of owning their work, and that they can take back what rightfully belongs to them.

# Rituals of the Eras Tour

For Taylor's fans, the Eras Tour was a true interactive experience. Audience members didn't just listen to her songs. They knew when to sing certain lyrics extra loud. They belted out chants that had been used on other tours and added new chants for Taylor's more recent songs. Sharing friendship bracelets became a big part of the tour.

Some fans made bracelets that spelled out lyrics from Taylor's songs, chants from the show, or other words that had special meanings. Fans made friends as they traded bracelets before and during the show. Afterward, they shared photos and videos of the bracelets they had collected on social media. The bracelets were a way of creating memories from the show of a lifetime.

Taylor has lived her life in front of the world, and it has not always been easy. She has gone through first loves and wrenching heartbreaks in public. When she put her life story and emotions into songs, some people laughed at her. Others, though, found comfort in knowing that someone else had the same feelings. There is something for everyone in Taylor's music. The internet is full of articles with titles like "A Taylor Swift Song for Every Situation" or "A Taylor Swift Lyric for Any Emotion."

Today, Taylor has moved on from or repaired relationships with many of the people she wrote about in her songs, including Katy Perry.

In May 2022, Taylor received an honorary Doctor of Fine Arts degree from New York University. She gave a speech to the graduates. Taylor talked about what she had learned as she grew up. She told the audience that they would make mistakes in life, just like she had.

But she explained that she had learned the most from her failures. She reminded the graduates that when people lose something, they often gain something, too.

Taylor's 2023 was filled with many big achievements. In October, she released the album *1989 (Taylor's Version)* and the Eras Tour movie. Both the album and film helped Taylor break several records. In December, she became the first living music artist to have five of their albums in the *Billboard*'s top ten list at the same time. That same month, the Eras Tour movie became the most successful concert film of all time. Because of her accomplishments, *TIME* magazine chose her as their Person of the Year.

College course about Taylor's songs

Taylor has been known as many things—country music singer, pop star, gossip magnet, business woman, cat lover, and best friend to her fans.

But she always thinks of herself as a songwriter first. For Taylor, it all started with words and her love of writing. Some college professors even teach courses where Taylor's lyrics are studied as literature and her albums are used to talk about different topics in psychology (the study of the ways that people think, feel, and behave).

Taylor's life has been its own form of literature—a very open book! She once said, "I always look at albums as chapters in my life. And to the fans, I'm so happy that you like this one. I'm so happy that this means that you liked this one. But I have to be really honest with you about something: I'm even more excited about the next chapter."

# Timeline of Taylor Swift's Life

| | |
|---|---|
| **1989** — | Taylor Swift is born on December 13 in West Reading, Pennsylvania |
| **2002** — | Begins to play the guitar and write songs |
| **2003** — | Signs development deal with RCA Records |
| — | Moves to Nashville |
| **2005** — | Signs record deal with Big Machine Records |
| **2006** — | Releases first album, titled *Taylor Swift* |
| **2008** — | Releases *Fearless* |
| **2010** — | Wins Album of the Year for *Fearless* at the Grammy Awards |
| — | Releases *Speak Now* |
| **2012** — | Releases *Red* |
| **2013** — | Opens the Taylor Swift Education Center in Nashville |
| **2014** — | Releases *1989* |
| **2017** — | Named a *TIME* magazine Person of the Year as one of the "Silence Breakers" |
| — | Releases *reputation* |
| **2019** — | Releases *Lover* |
| **2020** — | Releases *folklore* and *evermore* |
| **2022** — | Releases *Midnights* |
| **2023** — | Begins Eras Tour |

# Timeline of the World

1989 — The Berlin Wall separating East and West Germany comes down

2001 — Terrorists hijack airplanes and crash them into the World Trade Center and the Pentagon

2005 — The first YouTube video is uploaded

2008 — *Iron Man*, the first movie in the Marvel Cinematic Universe, is released

2009 — Barack Obama is inaugurated as the forty-fourth president of the United States

2012 — *Encyclopaedia Britannica* ends its print edition to become online only

2014 — Malaysia Aircraft Flight 370 disappears

2017 — Around five hundred thousand people take part in the Women's March in Washington, DC

2018 — Scientists find evidence of a body of water on Mars

2019 — Maine becomes the first state to ban Styrofoam containers

2020 — The COVID-19 pandemic spreads around the world

2021 — Juneteenth becomes a federal holiday

2022 — Russia invades Ukraine

2023 — The USDA approves the first vaccine for insects to protect honeybees from a deadly disease

# Bibliography

Aguirre, Abby. "Taylor Swift on Sexism, Scrutiny, and Standing Up for Herself." *Vogue*, August 8, 2019. https://www.vogue.com/article/taylor-swift-cover-september-2019.

Eells, Josh. "The Reinvention of Taylor Swift." *Rolling Stone*, September 8, 2014. https://www.rollingstone.com/music/music-news/the-reinvention-of-taylor-swift-116925/.

Hiatt, Brian. "Taylor Swift in Wonderland." *Rolling Stone*, October 25, 2012. https://www.rollingstone.com/music/music-news/taylor-swift-in-wonderland-180107/.

Hiatt, Brian. "Taylor Swift: The Rolling Stone Interview." *Rolling Stone*, September 18, 2019. https://www.rollingstone.com/music/music-features/taylor-swift-rolling-stone-interview-880794/.

Klosterman, Chuck. "Taylor Swift on 'Bad Blood,' Kanye West, and How People Interpret Her Lyrics." *GQ*, October 15, 2015. https://www.gq.com/story/taylor-swift-gq-cover-story.

Mischer, Don, and Ryan Polito, directors. *Journey to Fearless*. Film Signal, Hasbro Studios, 2010. 2 hr., 11 min.

Raab, Scott. "Why Taylor Swift Welcomed You to New York." *Esquire*, October 20, 2014. https://classic.esquire.com/article/2014/11/1/taylor-swift.

Snapes, Laura. "Taylor Swift: 'I Was Literally About to Break.' " *The Guardian*, August 24, 2019. https://www.theguardian.com/music/2019/aug/24/taylor-swift-pop-music-hunger-games-gladiators.

Stubbs, Dan. "Taylor Swift: Power, Fame and the Future." *NME*, October 9, 2015. https://www.nme.com/features/taylor-swift-power-fame-and-the-future-the-full-nme-cover-interview-549.

Swift, Taylor. "30 Things I Learned Before Turning 30." *Elle*, March 6, 2019. https://www.elle.com/culture/celebrities/a26628467/taylor-swift-30th-birthday-lessons/.

Wilson, Lana, director. *Miss Americana*. Tremolo Productions, 2020. 1 hr., 25 min. https://www.netflix.com/title/81028336.